:OFF!

CHECK OUT WHAT'S INSIDE!

FOOTY FUN!

It's all kicking off as Match of the Day picks out some footy rumbles!

BIG, BAD BUST-UPS!

Check me out on page 36!

ACE QUIZZES!

MYSTERY STARS!

Are these **10** Prem players dressing up for the winter?
You get a point for each right answer!

BBC EXPERTS!

Alan Shearer's Top 5...

GOAL KINGS!

MATCH OF THE DAY EXPERT!

Check out my top five goalscorers!

FERNANDO TORRES!

SHEARER SAYS: "Torres had a cracking first season at Liverpool! He came in with a lot to prove and had a big price tag, but it never affected him and he always pops up with a goal!"

SUPER STRIKER!

DAVID VILLA!

SHEARER SAYS: "I knew about him before Euro 2008, but he was sensational for Spain at the tournament! He was one of the best players there. He's a very good finisher and is incredibly quick!"

QUALITY FINISHER!

WAYNE ROONEY!

SHEARER SAYS: "I'm a huge fan of Rooney! He's got great ability, he's still young and still getting better. He can play in lots of positions, but I like it when he plays just off the main striker!"

LOVES SCORING!

THIERRY HENRY!

SHEARER SAYS: "I know how

GOAL MACHINE!

CRISTIANO RONALDO!

SHEARER SAYS: "Ronaldo has everything – he can score from long range, with both feet...

JET BUSTER!

MY SCORE
TOTAL SCORE

PLUS LOADS MORE!

10 TOP FO

Boost your footy knowledge with these great brain-busting facts!

1 Barcelona's Nou Camp stadium is the biggest in Europe. It holds 98,772 people!

THAT'S MASSIVE!

FCB

5 In 2006, Theo Walcott became the youngest player to play for England. He was only 17 at the time!

ENGLAND

ENGLAND U21

ENGLAND'S YOUNGEST STAR!

6 Brazil have won the World Cup a record five times!

BRILLIANT BRAZIL!

OTY FACTS!

3 Everton used to play their home games at Anfield – the current home of big city rivals Liverpool!

Everton 18 78

2 Real Madrid are the most successful European club side ever. They've been champions of Europe nine times!

4 Chelsea's table-topping 95 points in the 2004-2005 season is a Premier League record!

7 Arsenal have been in the top English division since 1919 – that's longer than any other team!

NOW BEAT THAT!

RECORD BREAKERS!

8 Tottenham were the first British team to win a European trophy. They won the European Cup Winners Cup in 1963!

FRENCH!

SCOTTISH!

9 No English manager has ever won the Premier League!

10 Man. United have won the FA Cup 11 times – that's a record!

BIG, BAD BUST

It's all kicking off a

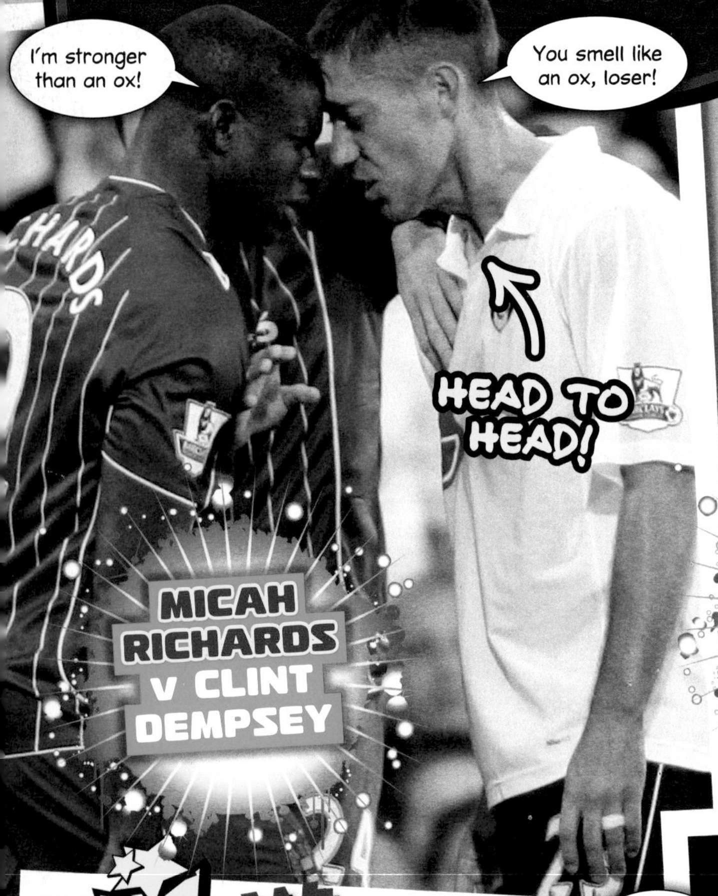

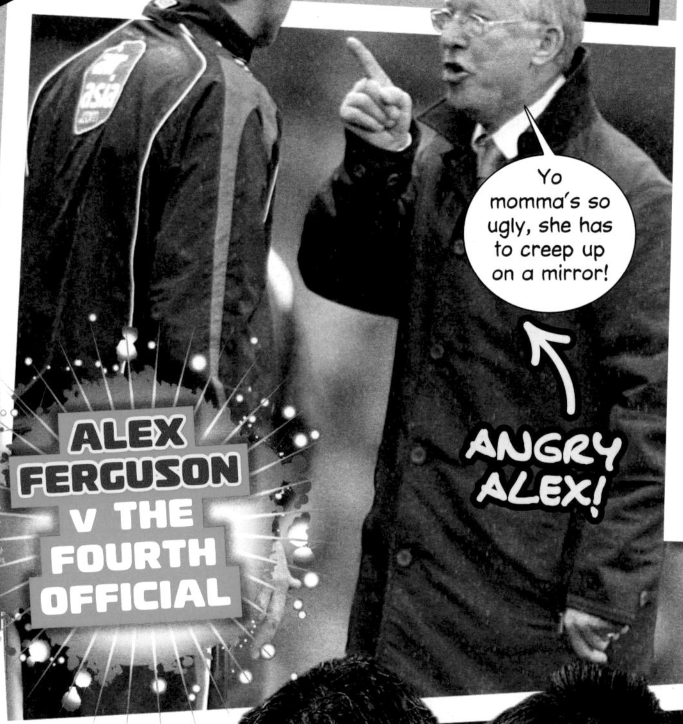

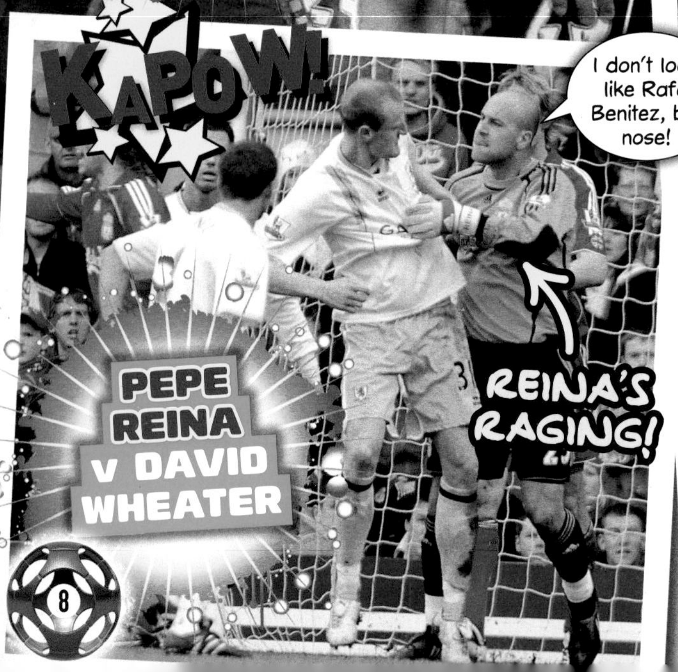

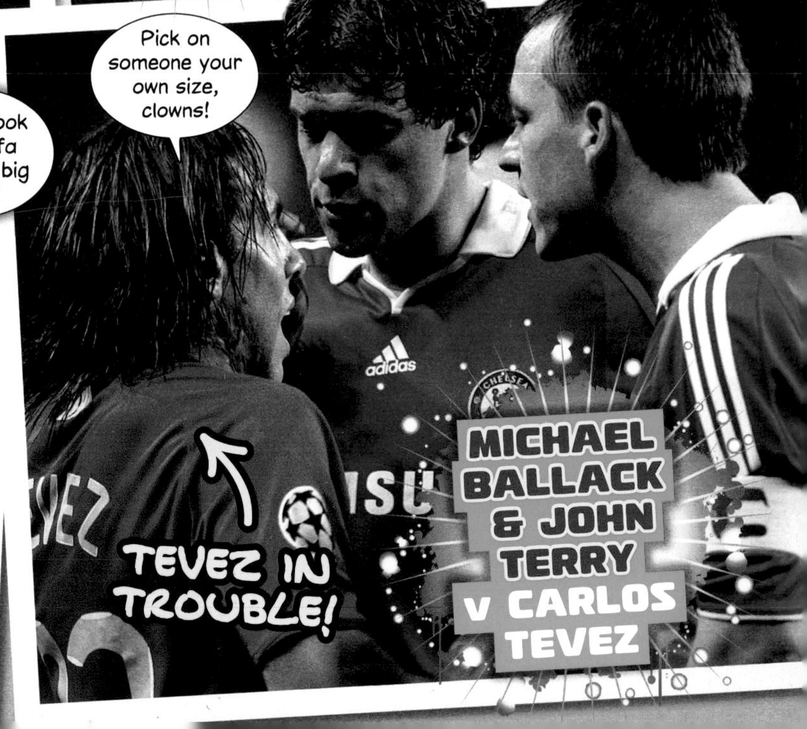

Alan Shearer's Top 5...
GOAL KINGS!

Check out my top five goalscorers!

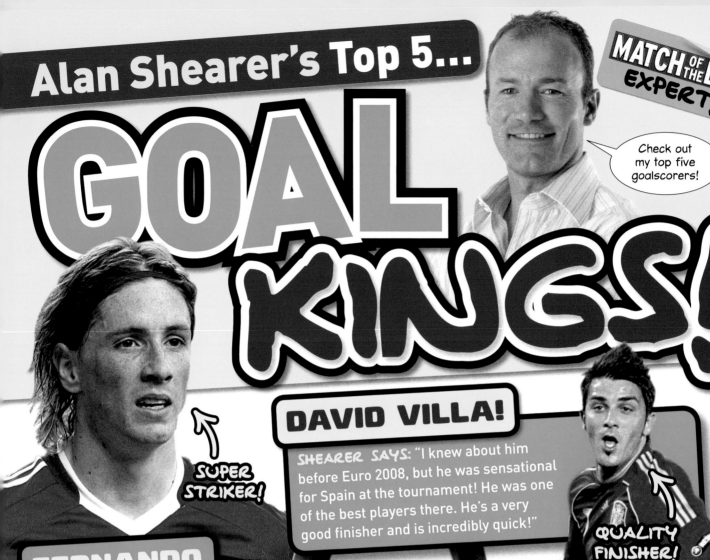

SUPER STRIKER!

DAVID VILLA!

SHEARER SAYS: "I knew about him before Euro 2008, but he was sensational for Spain at the tournament! He was one of the best players there. He's a very good finisher and is incredibly quick!"

QUALITY FINISHER!

FERNANDO TORRES!

SHEARER SAYS: "Torres had a cracking first season at Liverpool! He came in with a lot to prove and had a big price tag, but it never affected him and he always pops up with a goal!"

LOVES SCORING!

WAYNE ROONEY!

SHEARER SAYS: "I'm a huge fan of Rooney! He's got great ability, he's still young and still getting better. He can play in lots of positions, but I like it when he plays just off the main striker!"

GOAL MACHINE!

CRISTIANO RONALDO!

SHEARER SAYS: "Ronaldo has everything – he can score from long range, with both feet and he's good in the air. He scored 42 goals last season, which was sensational!"

NET BUSTER!

THIERRY HENRY!

SHEARER SAYS: "I know he struggled a bit at Barcelona last season, but he's still a top player. I remember how many goals he scored for Arsenal and the impact he had in England!"

WAYNE ROONEY

MAN. UNITED

Wayne scored an ace hat-trick on his debut for Man. United in 2004 against Fenerbahce!

MATCH OF THE **DAY** MAGAZINE

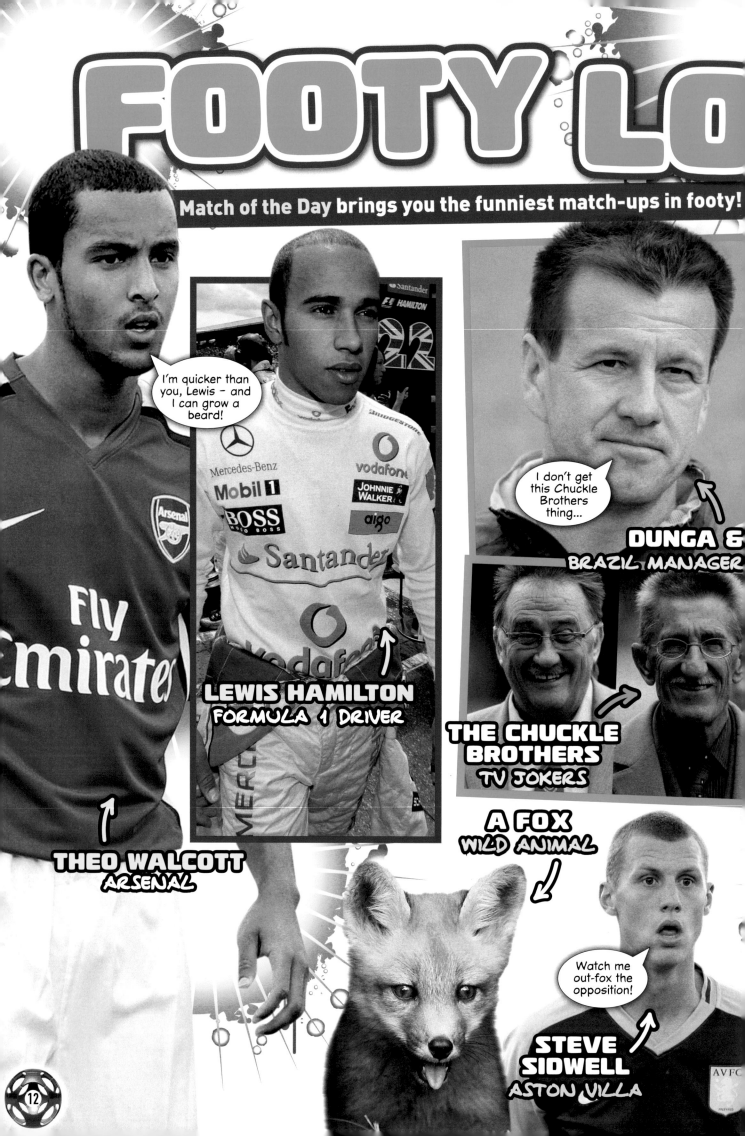

MOTTY'S QUIZ!

10 QUESTIONS ON...

ENGLAND!

Grab a point for each one you get right!

1 In which stadium do England play their home games?

YOU SAY ....

2 Which Prem striker has scored the most goals for the Three Lions?

YOU SAY ....

3 True or false? Steven Gerrard has won more caps than John Terry.

YOU SAY ....

4 Which Prem club does England star Rio Ferdinand play for?

YOU SAY ....

5 Which Arsenal star played for England before his Prem debut?

YOU SAY ....

6 Which midfielder won his 100th cap in 2008?

YOU SAY ....

7 How old was striker Wayne Rooney when he made his debut for England – 16, 17 or 18?

YOU SAY ....

8 Where did England winger David Bentley begin his career – Fulham, QPR or Arsenal?

YOU SAY ....

9 Can you name the Portsmouth keeper who is a regular in the England team?

YOU SAY ....

10 Who has scored more goals for England – Frank Lampard or Joe Cole?

YOU SAY ....

MY SCORE... OUT OF 10

14

ANSWERS (DON'T CHEAT!)

MORE QUIZ FUN ON PAGE 22!

MICHAEL BALLACK

CHELSEA

PREMIER LEAGUE HERO!

Midfield master Ballack scored seven goals in just 18 Premier League games last season!

MATCH OF THE **DAY**
MAGAZINE

Man. United win the Premier League again in 1997!

We did it again boys!

Gimme that trophy, kid!

Have some of this!

David goes to the 1998 World Cup with England! He scores a free-kick against Colombia but then gets sent off against Argentina, and England go out!

Oh nuts!

Becks helps United to make history! They win the treble – the Prem, FA Cup and Champions League – in 1999!

Yeeessss!

I hope I remember the words to the National Anthem!

In November 2000 he's made England captain for the first time, in a friendly against Italy!

United win the Prem again in 2001!

This makes up for being bald!

I've done this before, you know!

Pack your bags, lads!

In October 2001 David scores with an incredible late free-kick for England against Greece to send the Three Lions to the 2002 World Cup!

READ PART TWO OF BECKHAM'S STORY ON PAGE 56!

17

RONALDINHO... HIP-HOP KING!

AC Milan star Ronaldinho loves stepping out dressed like a rapper – but is he any good at rappin'?

What's going on with... England?

ASHLEY YOUNG

ASTON VILLA

PREMIER LEAGUE HERO!

Ashley scored nine goals and made 17 assists in the Premier League last season!

MATCH OF THE **DAY**
MAGAZINE

SUPER Skills!

HOW TO BE

PLAYER WATCH!

Don't forget these top keepers!

Learn how to be a safe pair of hands like Italy's *GIANLUIGI BUFFON*!

1 DAVID JAMES PORTSMOUTH

TOP SKILL: GREAT REFLEXES!

2 EDWIN VAN DER SAR MAN. UNITED

TOP SKILL: GRABBING CROSSES!

3 IKER CASILLAS REAL MADRID

TOP SKILL: SAVING PENALTIES!

4 ARTUR BORUC CELTIC

TOP SKILL: SHOUTING ORDERS!

5 PETR CECH CHELSEA

TOP SKILL: BRAVERY!

1 Shout at your team-mates to tell them if there's a player that they should be marking...

You have a better view than they do!

2 When you make a save, push the ball away from the goal so an attacker can't get the rebound.

Be strong when you knock the ball wide!

3

4

A QUALITY KEEPER!

When facing a penalty, focus on the ball and stand in the centre of the goal.

Use your arms to make yourself look really big!

When a striker is through on goal, put him off by running out as quickly as you can.

Be brave and go for the ball!

NOTHING GETS PAST BUFFON!

WICKED WORDSEARCH!

TOP STOPPERS!

How many of these top Prem keepers can you find?

```
Y J Z Q N H O P B X C I V Y S
K Q H H O W A R D J I S D K G
L N Z N A F A Q I P A V I R U
X T H B L V F U K H W M O S Y
D M H H M R A R W A R C Y C Q
R Z W D U R Q N L R B K T H K
R E P R N N K S D T I L A W R
O A I G I Z J A M E S P L A H
K S W N A E J G K X R E W R N
Y H F O A R T A U Y D S M Z L
G I V E N F K Z G E I C A E M
T A W V J Z H V I S H E W R U
G F J Q P S W R V C J A T K X
K E M F J Q F Q E S Z M T M W
Y V L B G U R C X N H D A H F
```

CECH

VAN DER SAR

ALMUNIA

- ☐ ALMUNIA
- ☐ **CECH**
- ☐ FRIEDEL
- ☐ **GIVEN**
- ☐ HART
- ☐ **HOWARD**
- ☐ JAMES
- ☐ **REINA**
- ☐ SCHWARZER
- ☐ **VAN DER SAR**

JAMES

GIVEN

HOWARD

MY SCORE... OUT OF 10

ANSWERS (DON'T CHEAT!)

MORE QUIZ FUN ON PAGE 30!

22

STEVEN GERRARD

LIVERPOOL

PLAYER WATCH!

Check out these five ace defenders!

1
RIO FERDINAND
MAN. UNITED
TOP SKILL: TACKLING!

2
JOHN TERRY
CHELSEA
TOP SKILL: BRAVERY!

3
FABIO CANNAVARO
REAL MADRID
TOP SKILL: POSITIONING!

4
GAEL CLICHY
ARSENAL
TOP SKILL: SPEED!

5
CARLOS PUYOL
BARCELONA
TOP SKILL: GREAT LEADER!

Learn how to play like Liverpool centre-back **JAMIE CARRAGHER!**

1

Stay on your feet and wait for the striker to show you enough of the ball – then you can take it off them!

Keep your eyes on the ball!

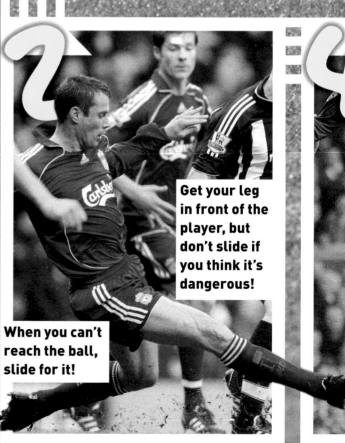

2

Get your leg in front of the player, but don't slide if you think it's dangerous!

When you can't reach the ball, slide for it!

3

4

ROCK SOLID DEFENDER!

CARRAGHER KNOWS WHEN TO PUT THE BOOT IN!

Launch a counter-attack by hitting the ball up the field after tackling someone!

Make sure you don't give the ball away though!

When marking a player at a corner, stand close and follow them around!

Try to jump higher than your opponent!

Jake Humphrey's Top 5...
MOMENTS OF 2008!

MATCH OF THE DAY EXPERT!

What a wicked year for football fans!

The BBC footy expert reveals the year's highlights!

RON'S THE BEST!

↑ **1**

CRISTIANO RONALDO!

JAKE SAYS: "I've never seen someone perform so well each week. That's what makes him so special. He scored 42 goals for Man. United last season and he's always a threat!"

TOP BOSS!

2

FABIO CAPELLO!

JAKE SAYS: "I was delighted when Fabio became the England manager. He'll get the best out of the players and make sure that England qualify for the 2010 World Cup!"

AWESOME ARSHAVIN!

3

EURO 2008!

JAKE SAYS: "It was a fantastic tournament full of attacking football, goals and top players like Russia's Andrei Arshavin. It was great to watch!"

4

POMPEY WIN THE CUP!

CRAZY FA CUP!

JAKE SAYS: "The FA Cup was full of shocks and surprises. Chasetown reached the Third Round, Barnsley knocked out Liverpool and Chelsea, and Portsmouth lifted the cup!"

CAN'T STOP SCORING!

5

FERNANDO TORRES!

JAKE SAYS: "I've never seen someone adapt so well to the Premier League! He links up brilliantly with Steven Gerrard, scores goals for fun and helped Spain to win Euro 2008!"

PHIL JAGIELKA

PREMIER LEAGUE HERO!

Fans' fave Jagielka joined Everton for a bargain £4 million from Sheffield United in 2007!

MATCH OF THE DAY MAGAZINE

HOW TO BEA

PLAYER WATCH!

Check out these ace midfielders!

Learn how to play like Chelsea and Germany ace MICHAEL BALLACK!

1 STEVEN GERRARD
LIVERPOOL

TOP SKILL: SHOOTING!

2 XAVI
BARCELONA
TOP SKILL: ACCURATE PASSING!

3 OWEN HARGREAVES
MAN. UNITED

TOP SKILL: TACKLING!

4 ANDREA PIRLO
AC MILAN

TOP SKILL: THROUGH-BALLS!

5 CESC FABREGAS
ARSENAL

TOP SKILL: CREATING GOALS!

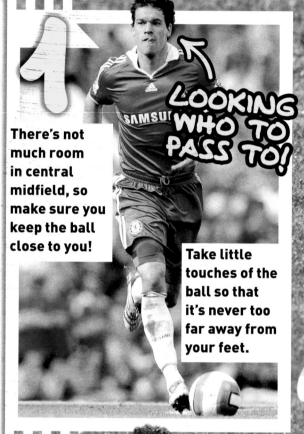

1

LOOKING WHO TO PASS TO!

There's not much room in central midfield, so make sure you keep the ball close to you!

Take little touches of the ball so that it's never too far away from your feet.

3

2

Try chipping the ball over the defence for a striker to run on to!

Chip the ball by getting your foot under it and following through with your leg.

4

28

AWESOME MIDFIELDER!

Use the side of your foot to play short passes – it's much more accurate!

Race back when the other team is attacking and stop them!

If you try a slide tackle you must get the ball before the player!

BALLACK BOSSES THE MIDFIELD!

MOTTY'S QUIZ!

10 QUESTIONS ON... SCOTLAND!

There's a point for each one you get right!

1 Which Prem club signed Scotland keeper Craig Gordon for £9m in 2007?

YOU SAY ....

2 In which year did captain Barry Ferguson make his debut – 1998, 2000 or 2002?

YOU SAY ....

3 Who did Scotland beat twice in their Euro 2008 qualifying campaign – France or Italy?

YOU SAY ....

4 With which club has midfield star Darren Fletcher won two Prem titles?

YOU SAY ....

5 Scotland's right-back left Rangers for Tottenham in 2008 – who is he?

YOU SAY ....

6 What's the name of Scotland's home ground – Hampden Park or Ibrox?

YOU SAY ....

7 What is Scotland's lowest ever FIFA world ranking – 64, 70, 78?

YOU SAY ....

8 Which current Scotland striker has played for both Celtic and Rangers?

YOU SAY ....

9 True or false? Scottish fans are known as the Tartan Army.

YOU SAY ....

10 When did Scotland last qualify for the World Cup – 2006, 2002 or 1998?

YOU SAY ....

MY SCORE... OUT OF 10

MORE QUIZ FUN ON PAGE 38!

30

THEO WALCOTT

ARSENAL

PREMIER LEAGUE HERO!

Wicked winger Walcott made his debut for the Gunners in 2006 when he was just 17 years old!

MATCH OF THE DAY MAGAZINE

PLAYER WATCH!

Check out these five wicked wingers!

1 NANI
MAN. UNITED

TOP SKILL:
SILKY STEPOVERS!

2 ASHLEY YOUNG
ASTON VILLA

TOP SKILL:
RAW SPEED!

3 DAVID SILVA
VALENCIA

TOP SKILL:
TIGHT CONTROL!

4 JOE COLE
CHELSEA

TOP SKILL:
CRAZY TRICKS!

5 WESLEY SNEIJDER
REAL MADRID

TOP SKILL:
ACE SHOOTING!

Learn how to play like Barcelona and Argentina ace *LIONEL MESSI*!

1

Messi is a master of close control, which makes it impossible for defenders to get the ball.

GENTLY DOES IT!

Take loads of light touches with the ball to make it easier to avoid tackles!

2

To really give the full-back nightmares you need to attack him on both sides.

Be strong on both feet – then he'll never know which way you're going!

A QUALITY WINGER!

If Messi spots space behind the defence, he can use his pace to get round the back.

Knock the ball past your man and set off on a sprint to beat him to it!

To be a really great winger you need to be a clinical finisher like Leo.

When you're past the last man, stay calm and side-foot the ball into the corner of the net!

MESSI THE MAGICIAN SCORES A SCORCHER!

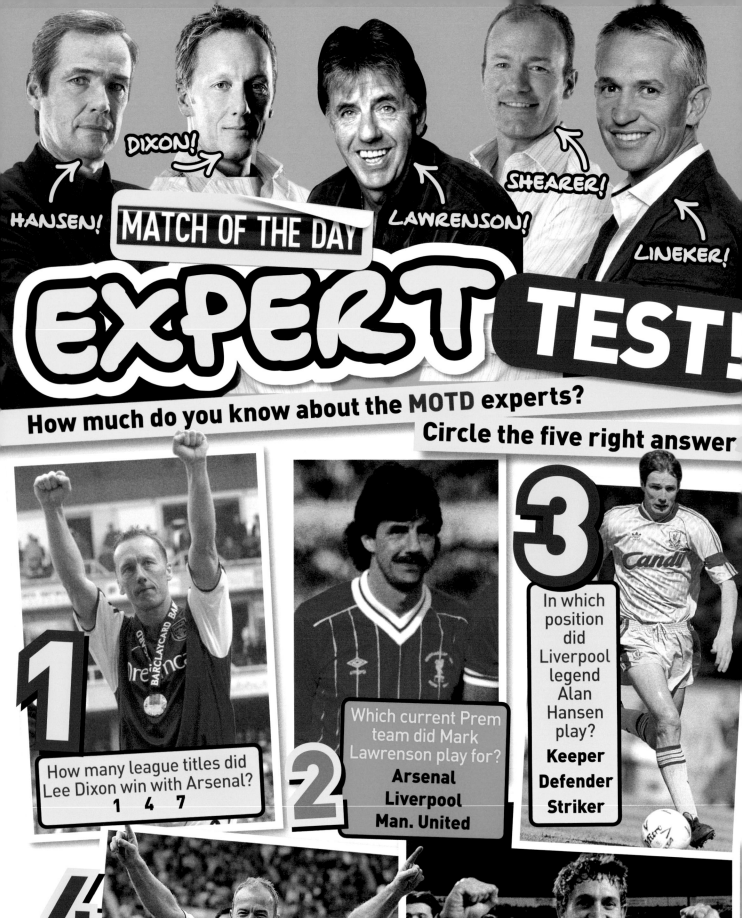

HANSEN!

DIXON!

LAWRENSON!

SHEARER!

LINEKER!

MATCH OF THE DAY
EXPERT TEST!

How much do you know about the MOTD experts?

Circle the five right answer

1 How many league titles did Lee Dixon win with Arsenal?
1   4   7

2 Which current Prem team did Mark Lawrenson play for?
Arsenal
Liverpool
Man. United

3 In which position did Liverpool legend Alan Hansen play?
Keeper
Defender
Striker

4 How much did Newcastle pay Blackburn for Alan Shearer in 1996?
£5m   £15m   £25m

5 How many World Cups did Gary Lineker play in for England?
0   2   4

34

ANSWERS (DON'T CHEAT!)

1 Four, 2 Liverpool, 3 Defender, 4 £15m, 5 Two

MICAH RICHARDS

MAN. CITY

SUPER Skills!

HOW TO BE

PLAYER WATCH!

Check out these five wicked strikers!

Learn how to play like Man. United and England hero WAYNE ROONEY!

1

YAKUBU
EVERTON

TOP SKILL: AWESOME POWER!

2

FERNANDO TORRES
LIVERPOOL

TOP SKILL: LETHAL FINISHING!

3

NICOLAS ANELKA
CHELSEA

TOP SKILL: BURNING PACE!

4

MIROSLAV KLOSE
BAYERN MUNICH

TOP SKILL: ACE HEADERS!

5

MICHAEL OWEN
NEWCASTLE

TOP SKILL: SHARP MOVEMENT!

1

Rooney's wicked vision and awareness give him an extra second to spot the perfect pass.

Keep your head up so you can spot a team-mate and think about your next move!

2

You need to get yourself ahead of the defender so you're first to the ball.

Use your body and strength as a shield to stop him getting a foot in!

A SUPER STRIKER!

When Rooney smashes a volley towards goal, there's no keeper in the world that can stop it!

Hit it with your laces and keep your body over the ball to stop it flying over!

The United superstar loves scoring with chips – it makes keepers look stupid!

Lean back a bit and stab your foot under the ball to impress your mates with a sweet lob!

WAZZA HAS THE LOT — POWER, PACE AND FLASH SKILLS!

MOTTY'S QUIZ!

10 QUESTIONS ON...

REP. OF IRELAND!

Test your Rep. of Ireland footy knowledge with these ace questions – give yourself a point for each one you get right!

1 True or false? The Rep. of Ireland made the World Cup quarter-finals in 1990.

YOU SAY ....

2 Who has scored more international goals – John O'Shea or Andy Reid?

YOU SAY ....

3 Name the Man. City captain who plays as a centre-back for the Rep. of Ireland.

YOU SAY ....

4 How many Prem clubs has winger Damien Duff played for – two, three or four?

YOU SAY ....

5 Winger Aiden McGeady plays in Scotland for which top club?

YOU SAY ....

6 Who did Stephen Hunt make his debut against – Russia or San Marino?

YOU SAY ....

7 Which Premier League club does record goalscorer Robbie Keane play for?

YOU SAY ....

8 Who is the Rep. of Ireland's Italian manager – Giovanni Trapattoni or Marcello Lippi?

YOU SAY ....

9 Stephen McPhail played for which Championship club in last year's FA Cup final?

YOU SAY ....

10 Which Newcastle keeper is the Rep. of Ireland's number one?

YOU SAY ....

MY SCORE... OUT OF 10

ANSWERS (DON'T CHEAT!)

1 True, 2 Andy Reid, 3 Richard Dunne, 4 Three, 5 Celtic, 6 San Marino, 7 Liverpool, 8 Giovanni Trapattoni, 9 Cardiff, 10 Shay Given

MORE QUIZ FUN ON PAGE 50!

STEVEN TAYLOR

PREMIER LEAGUE HERO!

Steven supported Newcastle as a kid and made his debut in 2004 when he was 18!

MATCH OF THE DAY MAGAZINE

The wicked career of...

RONA

Cristiano Ronaldo has had an awesome caree
– **Match of the Day** checks out the winger's be

DREAM DEBUT!

Sporting Lisbon scouts spotted Ronny when he was just 13 years old and they didn't waste any time snapping him up. He made his first-team debut as a 16-year-old in 2001, smashing in two goals to lead Sporting to victory!

CRISTIANO RONALDO

Age: 23 Position: Winger Country: Portugal Value: £60 million

RONNY AT 16!

FIRST TOURNAMENT WITH PORTUGAL!

WANTED!

Prem clubs started buzzing round Ronaldo after he rocked for Portugal in UEFA's Under-17 Euro Championship. The wicked winger was the star of the tournament and started attracting interest from Liverpool!

LDO

RON'S PREM STATS!

2003-4
APPEARANCES: 29
GOALS: 4

2004-5
APPEARANCES: 33
GOALS: 5

2005-6
APPEARANCES: 33
GOALS: 9

2006-7
APPEARANCES: 34
GOALS: 17

2007-8
APPEARANCES: 34
GOALS: 31

TURN OVER FOR MORE RONALDO!

ready its!

UNITED SWOOP!

In 2003 Sporting played Man. United in a friendly and Ronaldo ripped them apart! Red Devils boss Alex Ferguson was so impressed with the Portugal star's amazing skills, he splashed out £12.24 million to bring him to Old Trafford!

PREM NEW BOY!

STRIKE ONE!

It didn't take long for Ronny to grab his first goal in the Prem! United fans were loving it when the new number seven whipped in an amazing free-kick in a 3-0 win against Portsmouth!

RONNY GETS OFF THE MARK!

CUP STAR!

TROPHY TIME!

Ronaldo stormed to FA Cup glory in 2004. His wicked header in the final set Man. United on the road to victory against Millwall and his first trophy in English footy!

ROCKIN' EURO FOOTY!

WHAT A SEASON!

UNITED'S MAIN MAN!

EURO STAR!

The king of tricks led Portugal all the way to the final of Euro 2004. In the end they were beaten by Greece – but Ronny made the team of the tournament!

PREM CHAMP!

Ronaldo was unstoppable as United became Premier League champions for the first time in four years in 2007 – his penalty at Man. City made sure of the title and he finished as the Red Devils' top scorer with 23 goals!

DOUBLE SCOOP!

2007 got even better for Ronny – his amazing form saw him scoop both the PFA Player of the Year and Young Player of the Year awards. He was the first footy star to do that since 1977!

HAT-TRICK HERO!

TOP TREBLE!

Cristiano racked up his first ever Man. United hat-trick against Newcastle in January 2008. The footy superstar got the ball rolling with a slick free-kick as United stuffed the Magpies 6-0!

UNSTOPPABLE!

BEST FREE-KICK EVER?

The Portuguese genius shook up the Prem with an unbelievable free-kick against Portsmouth! His shot dipped like an arrow into the net – Alex Ferguson reckons it was the best free-kick ever!

MR INCREDIBLE

Ronny proved himself as the world's most amazing footy hero in 2008. He thumped in an astonishing 42 goals for United, picked up another Prem trophy and topped it off with his first ever Champions League title!

TITLE NUMBER TWO!

GOAL MACHINE!

KING OF EUROPE!

FOOTY MAD!

The Prem stars are having their big Christmas party!

Harry Redknapp and Peter Crouch are hosting a Christmas fancy dress party...

That'll be the first of the guests, Crouchy!

I can't wait, Harry! Or should I call you Potter?

Torres and Gerrard are first to arrive...

He was meant to be Robin – but he messed up!

Who are you, Fernando?

A few minutes later and the next guests arrive...

Aaron Lennon and Jermain Defoe! What are you two?

And I'm you, Crouchy! Ooh, I'm so tall!

I'm Jonathan Woodgate! Get it?

Have you come as a diver, Crouchy!

WOBBLE!!!

Aaarrrrgghhh!

Nah, I've come as Didier Drogba!

The lads are having a wicked time...

FLAP! FLAP!

Is that all the guests?

GLUG!

No! Carlos Tevez ain't here yet!

The door bell has just rung...

DING-DONG!

Am I late, Harry?

Err... not really, Carlos! But what are you wearing?

The invitation said to wear a fancy dress!

No, Carlos! It said to come in fancy dress!

44

JERMAINE JENAS

TOTTENHAM

PREMIER LEAGUE HERO!

Jermaine was named vice captain of Tottenham last summer by manager Juande Ramos!

MATCH OF THE DAY MAGAZINE

MATCH OF THE DAY'S GOALS OF THE SEASON!

Check out these super strikes from last term – picked out by the BBC footy experts!

FROM THE HALFWAY LINE!

APRIL
Stiliyan Petrov
Derby v ASTON VILLA

The Villa midfielder smacked the ball from the centre circle with his left foot, and it flew over the Derby keeper!

Cristiano Ronaldo
MAN. UNITED v Aston Villa

Ronaldo's clever backheel flick in the box was awesome! It caught the Villa defenders by surprise and gave the keeper no chance at all!

BRILL BACKHEEL!

FEBRUARY

Daryl Murphy
SUNDERLAND v Wigan

Murphy's magical strike from the edge of the area rocketed into the top corner and nearly ripped the net off!

WHAT A SCORCHER!

BEST FREE-KICK EVER?

JANUARY
Cristiano Ronaldo
MAN. UNITED v Portsmouth

This free-kick was one of the best ever! Ronaldo blasted it over the Pompey wall and it sailed into the net in the blink of an eye!

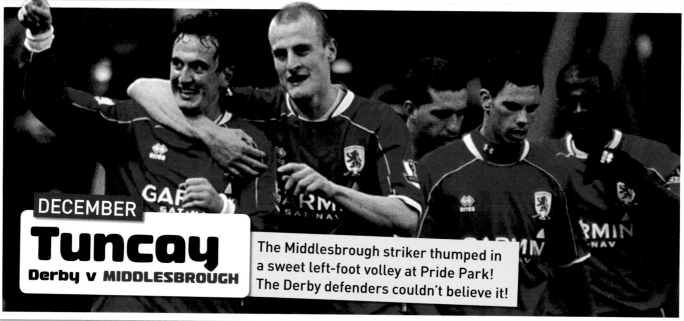

DECEMBER
Tuncay
Derby v MIDDLESBROUGH

The Middlesbrough striker thumped in a sweet left-foot volley at Pride Park! The Derby defenders couldn't believe it!

OCTOBER
Carlos Tevez
MAN. UTD v Middlesbrough

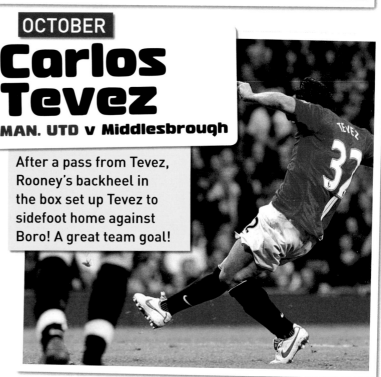

After a pass from Tevez, Rooney's backheel in the box set up Tevez to sidefoot home against Boro! A great team goal!

NOVEMBER
Luke Young
MIDDLESBROUGH v Tottenham

Young's only scored a few goals in his whole career – and this long-range beauty was incredible! It was against his old club, too!

VOLLEY TO VICTORY!

MATCH OF THE **DAY** **GOAL OF THE SEASON!**

SEPTEMBER

Emmanuel Adebayor
Tottenham v ARSENAL

For his second goal of the match, the Arsenal striker flicked the ball up and blasted an unstoppable volley into the top corner!

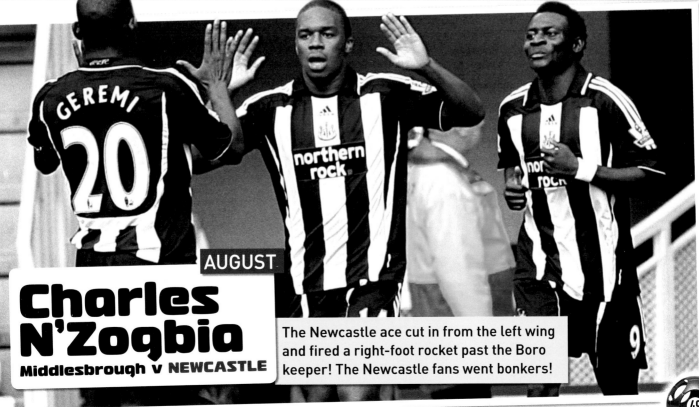

AUGUST

Charles N'Zogbia
Middlesbrough v NEWCASTLE

The Newcastle ace cut in from the left wing and fired a right-foot rocket past the Boro keeper! The Newcastle fans went bonkers!

MOTTY'S QUIZ!
SPOT THE STARS!

10 Prem stars are hiding in the crowd – can you find them? Grab a point for each one you find!

- ☐ **DEAN ASHTON**
- ☐ **GARETH BARRY**
- ☐ **DECO**
- ☐ **STEWART DOWNING**
- ☐ **CESC FABREGAS**
- ☐ **JO**
- ☐ **JOLEON LESCOTT**
- ☐ **LUKA MODRIC**
- ☐ **PETER CROUCH**
- ☐ **WAYNE ROONEY**

ANSWERS

MY SCORE...

OUT OF 10

MORE QUIZ FUN ON PAGE 58!

PETER CROUCH

PREMIER LEAGUE HERO!

Crouchy became Pompey's record signing when he joined from Liverpool for £11 million!

MATCH OF THE **DAY** MAGAZINE

TOP 5 FOOTY SCARECUTS!

Match of the Day reveals the worst haircuts in the world of footy!

MOP HEAD!

I can clean the floor with this!

SPAGHETTI HAIR!

Hmmm. My hair tastes nice!

1 CARLOS PUYOL Barcelona

2 BACARY SAGNA Arsenal

GIRLY PIGTAILS!

3 ABEL XAVIER LA Galaxy

4 STEVEN PIENAAR Everton

RIDICULOUS FRINGE!

SHEEP HEAD!

5 LOCO Angola

Baah! Baah!

FLASHBACK! David Beckham

Woah! Check out David Beckham's hair when he was 11! Not cool, Becks!

DEAN ASHTON

PREMIER LEAGUE HERO!

Dean scored twice inside the opening ten minutes of the 2008-09 season!

MATCH OF THE DAY MAGAZINE

PART 2

THE AMAZING LIFE STORY OF DAVID BECKHAM!

David helps England to the quarter-finals of the 2002 World Cup, but they can't get past Brazil!

I can't watch. Tell me when it's over!

I love this trophy!

Becks gets his hands on the Prem trophy for the last time in 2003...

...and soon after he joins Real Madrid for £24 million in June 2003!

Who's the old guy?

BECKHAM 23

That'll come down with snow on!

Yeah!

A year later he's off to Euro 2004 with England, but Portugal put an end to his Euro dream in a quarter-final penalty shoot-out!

Oomph, get in!

I hate penalties against Portugal!

Hug me!

David becomes the first English player to score at three different World Cups, when he scores England's winner against Ecuador at the 2006 World Cup! But England are dumped out by Portugal in the quarter-finals!

He steps down as England captain after the World Cup!

...one last thing – what hairstyle should I have next?

David wins his first trophy in Spain when he picks up La Liga with Real Madrid in 2007!

Ha, ha! Stop mucking about Ruud!

This trophy is too big!

Dude, it rains paper in America!

BECKHAM 23

That's confetti, David!

He makes a stunning move to American team LA Galaxy soon after. They're really happy to sign him!

Thanks fans!

Très bien, monsieur!

Well played Becks!

Becks wins his 100th England cap in March 2008 when he plays in a friendly against France!

BENTLE

Soon after, he turns the clock back 12 years by scoring from the halfway line again!

Show me how to do that!

Easy! Easy! Easy!

Captain Becks is back!

Here's the armband David!

BECKHAM

England boss Fabio Capello gives Beckham the captain's armband for a friendly against Trinidad & Tobago.

THE END... FOR NOW!

57

WALES!

Grab a point for each correct answer!

1 Where did Arsenal sign Wales superkid Aaron Ramsey from?

YOU SAY ....

2 How many current Prem clubs has Craig Bellamy played for – 2, 3 or 4?

YOU SAY ....

3 Which Prem club did Wales full-back Chris Gunter sign for in January 2008?

YOU SAY ....

4 True or False? Joe Ledley has also played for Wales at U-17, U-19 and U-21 levels!

YOU SAY ....

5 In which stadium do Wales play their home games?

YOU SAY ....

6 How many times have Wales qualified for the World Cup?

YOU SAY ....

7 Which Man. United winger retired from playing for Wales in 2007?

YOU SAY ....

8 Which La Liga side has Wales boss John Toshack managed – Real Madrid or Barcelona?

YOU SAY ....

9 Which Wigan midfielder is Wales' playmaker and set-piece specialist?

YOU SAY ....

10 On his Wales debut, keeper Wayne Hennessey was – 18, 20 or 22?

YOU SAY ....

MY SCORE... OUT OF 10

MORE QUIZ FUN ON PAGE 70!

58

DEAN WHITEHEAD

PREMIER LEAGUE HERO!

The Sunderland skipper joined the club for a bargain £150,000 from Oxford in 2004!

MATCH OF THE DAY MAGAZINE

BEHIND THE SCENES AT MATCH OF THE DAY!

Check out what goes on behind the TV cameras at Match of the Day!

BBC STUDIO!
Match of the Day is filmed at the BBC's massive television studios in West London! The programme was first shown back in 1964!

LAWRENSON!

Television Centre

FOOTY CRAZY!
The presenters have a meeting to get ready for the show in the afternoon, then watch the action live on TV!

TV CENTRE!

CHILL OUT!

Lineker and the lads like to be comfortable when they're watching! Look at Lee Dixon making his notes!

DIXON!

LOADS OF TVs!

Check out all the TVs the presenters watch! They can see every live game at the same time – it really is the ultimate football fan's dream!

TECHNICAL TIME!

This is where *MOTD* is controlled and the presenters and cameramen get told what to do! It looks really complicated with all the switches!

FINAL WHISTLE!

When the games finish, the action is then edited on these special machines. It can be pretty tricky to get all the best bits in!

REHEARSALS!

Gary Lineker is ready in the studio before the show goes live on Saturday night. He checks all his notes and prepares to introduce the first game!

GETTING MAKE-UP!

The presenters have to have make-up put on before the show starts because the huge lights in the TV studio reflect off their faces!

SHEARER!

ON AIR!

The cameras are on and the show begins! *Match of the Day* fans can settle down and watch all the best action from every Prem game!

LINEKER!

TURN OVER FOR LINEKER'S ACE FOOTY CAREER!

61

GARY LINEKER...
FOOTY LEGEND!

Check out the wicked footy career of Match of the Day star Gary Lineker!

TOP TOFFEE!

Champions Everton snapped Gary up in 1985! The striker was red-hot at Goodison Park, scoring 30 league goals in one season to help Everton finish runners-up in both the league and the FA Cup in 1986!

CLUB: LEICESTER
DATE: 1977 TO 1985
COST: FREE

CLUB: EVERTON
DATE: 1985 TO 1986
COST: £850,000

GOAL MACHINE GARY!

LEICESTER LAD!

Gary signed professional forms with his local team Leicester City after leaving school in 1977. When he was 18 he made his debut and quickly became a lethal striker. He cracked in 95 goals in his time with the club!

BARCA BOY!

fter one season at Everton, La Liga iants Barcelona paid a mega £2.75 million for Gary. He bagged 44 goals or the club and became a hero when e scored a hat-trick against arch-ivals Real Madrid!

CLUB: BARCELONA
DATE: 1986 TO 1989
COST: £2.75 MILLION

JAPAN JOURNEY!

Gary made a shock move to play for Grampus Eight in Japan in 1993! He didn't score so many goals there and struggled with injury, but he was still one of the best players in the new J League before retiring in 1994!

CLUB: TOTTENHAM
DATE: 1989 TO 1992
COST: £1.1 MILLION

SPURS STAR!

Lineker came back to England in 1989 to lead Tottenham's attack! He continued to smack in the goals – scoring 67 in 105 games – and helped the London club to win the FA Cup in 1991!

CLUB: GRAMPUS EIGHT
DATE: 1993 TO 1994
COST: FREE

THREE LIONS HERO!

ENGLAND ACE!

Gary made his England debut in 1984 and went on to score an amazing 48 goals in just 80 games for his country! He was the top scorer at the 1986 World Cup and fired England to the semi-final four years later in Italy!

MOTD STARS... AS FOOTY HEROES!

ALAN SHEARER!
Alan was a goal machine for Newcastle!

MARK LAWRENSON!
Defender Lawro helped Liverpool to five league titles!

ALAN HANSEN!
Al won 22 trophies as a Liverpool centre-back!

LEE DIXON!
Right-back Lee was an Arsenal star for 14 years!

WHEN KEEPERS ATTACK!

The big lesson here is don't mess with goalkeepers – they're mental!

CRASH!
ARTUR BORUC
CELTIC v Hearts

SHUSAKU NISHIKAWA
JAPAN v Cameroon

BANG!

CRUNCH!
MARKUS HORISON
INDONESIA v South Korea

ANDREIA
BRAZIL WOMEN v Australia Women

WALLOP!

EDWIN VAN DER SAR
MAN. UNITED v Chelsea

SMACK!

KAPOW!
KONSTANTINOS CHALKIAS
GREECE v Norway

DAVID WHEATER

MIDDLESBROUGH

PREMIER LEAGUE HERO!

The big centre-back made his Boro debut as an 18-year-old in the UEFA Cup in 2005!

MATCH OF THE DAY MAGAZINE

PREM REC

Match of the Day reveals the Premier League's top record-breakers!

OLDEST CLUB!

Stoke are the oldest club to have ever played in the Prem. They started in 1863!

In the 2006-07 season, Man. City set the record for the least home goals scored – they only bagged ten goals at the City of Manchester stadium!

SCORED THE MOST!

MOST WINS IN A SEASON!

Match of the Day expert Alan Shearer scored 260 Prem goals in his career! That's way more than anyone else!

Chelsea have won more games in a Prem season than anyone else! They won 29 games on their way to winning the title in 2004-05 and 2005-06!

...ORDS!

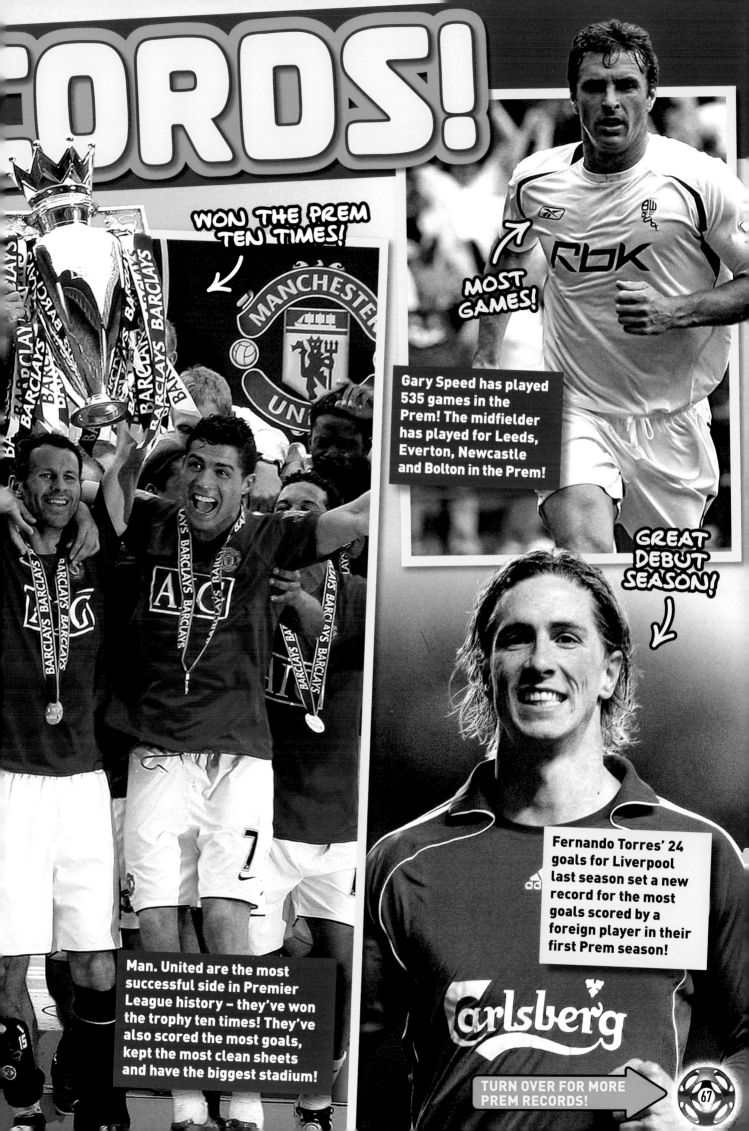

WON THE PREM TEN TIMES!

MOST GAMES!

Gary Speed has played 535 games in the Prem! The midfielder has played for Leeds, Everton, Newcastle and Bolton in the Prem!

GREAT DEBUT SEASON!

Fernando Torres' 24 goals for Liverpool last season set a new record for the most goals scored by a foreign player in their first Prem season!

Man. United are the most successful side in Premier League history – they've won the trophy ten times! They've also scored the most goals, kept the most clean sheets and have the biggest stadium!

TURN OVER FOR MORE PREM RECORDS!

PREM RECORDS!

RELEGATED THE MOST!

Crystal Palace have been relegated from the Prem the most! They've dropped out of the league four times – in 1993, 1995, 1998 and 2005!

Cristiano Ronaldo has scored more goals in a season than any other Prem midfielder! The wicked winger scored 31 goals for Man. United last season!

GOAL MACHINE!

MOST FOULS!

Arsenal are the only side to go through a Prem season without losing a match! They went through the 2003-04 season without losing and won the league title!

Bolton's tough striker Kevin Davies has made over 500 fouls! He committed more fouls than any other player in the 2004-05, 2005-06 and 2006-07 seasons!

PREM GIANT!

American keeper Ian Feuer is the tallest to ever play in the Prem! He was 2cm taller than Peter Crouch when he played four games for West Ham in 2000!

SMALLEST PLAYER!

Ex-Tottenham winger Jose Dominguez is still the smallest to ever play in the Prem! He was even 5cm smaller than Aaron Lennon at 5ft 5ins – Spurs love their small wingers!

WORST TEAM!

Derby became the worst team in the league's history last season – they only picked up 11 points and won just one game in 38 matches!

PROMOTED TO PREM THE MOST!

Sunderland have been promoted to the Prem four times! They finished top of the Championship in 1996, 1999, 2005 and 2007.

UNBEATABLE ARSENAL!

HIGHEST SCORING DEFENDER!

Joleon Lescott has scored more goals than any other defender in a Prem season – he netted ten goals for Everton last season!

GUESS WHO!

Can you name these **10** footy stars in action? Take a point for each one!

1

2

3

4

5

6

7

8

9

10

MY SCORE... OUT OF **10**

ANSWERS (DON'T CHEAT)

MORE QUIZ FUN ON PAGE 78!

ROMAN BEDNAR

WEST BROM

PREMIER LEAGUE HERO!

The Czech Republic striker bagged 13 league goals to get West Brom promoted last season!

MATCH OF THE DAY MAGAZINE

MAN. UN

THE BEST NAMES IN FOOTY!

Get ready lads – it's gonna be a loud one!

Check out the crazy names of these ace footy stars from around the world!

DEAN WINDASS

Club: Hull
Age: 39
Position: Striker
Country: England

JET POWERED!

BRIGHT LAD!

Seems like I'm always playing in a Sunday League!

UNSTOPPABLE!

Extra time? Bring it on!

SUNNY SUNDAY

Club: Valencia
Age: 20
Position: Midfielder
Country: Spain

ENERGY MURAMBADORO

Club: Bidvest Wits
Age: 26
Position: Goalkeeper
Country: Zimbabwe

Caught the keeper off his line again!

STUNNER!

Call that a foul? You're having a laugh ref!

TEAM JOKER!

MANAGER'S PET!

My favourite film? *Ratatouille,* of course!

SURPRISE MORIRI

Club: Mamelodi Sundowns
Age: 28
Position: Striker
Country: South Africa

LAUGHTER CHILEMBE

Club: CAPS United
Age: 32
Position: Defender
Country: Zambia

RAZVAN RAT

Club: Shakhtar Donetsk
Age: 27
Position: Defender
Country: Romania

What's going on at... Man. United?

Alex Ferguson has called Wayne Rooney into his office...

Right then, Wayne! We've got a big game on Saturday!

Yeah, boss!

It'll help us if you go away and learn about the tactics!

No probs, boss! Leave it to me!

The next day...

A pack weighs 15 to 18 grams and contains about 36 sweets...

Tactics, Wayne! Not *Tic Tacs!*

MORTEN PEDERSEN

PREMIER LEAGUE HERO!

The wicked winger only missed one Prem game for Blackburn in the 2007–2008 season!

MATCH OF THE DAY
MAGAZINE

TWO FAMOUS OWNERS!

Liam Ridgewell
Birmingham

LIAM SAYS: "He's a Bulldog called Bruno! I got him from Juan Pablo Angel when we were at Aston Villa together. He had a couple, so I took one off his hands!"

BRASS THE LAB!

Mikel Arteta
Everton

MIKEL SAYS: "I've got a Labrador called Brass! My uncle used to have a dog with that name, so we decided we were going to keep it going in the family!"

"MEAN
DO

These footy stars love

Dean Whitehead
Sunderland

DEAN SAYS: "I own a Pug dog which is called Faffi! I love Pugs because they're pretty cool-looking little dogs. Don't you think so?"

BARKING MAD PUG FANS

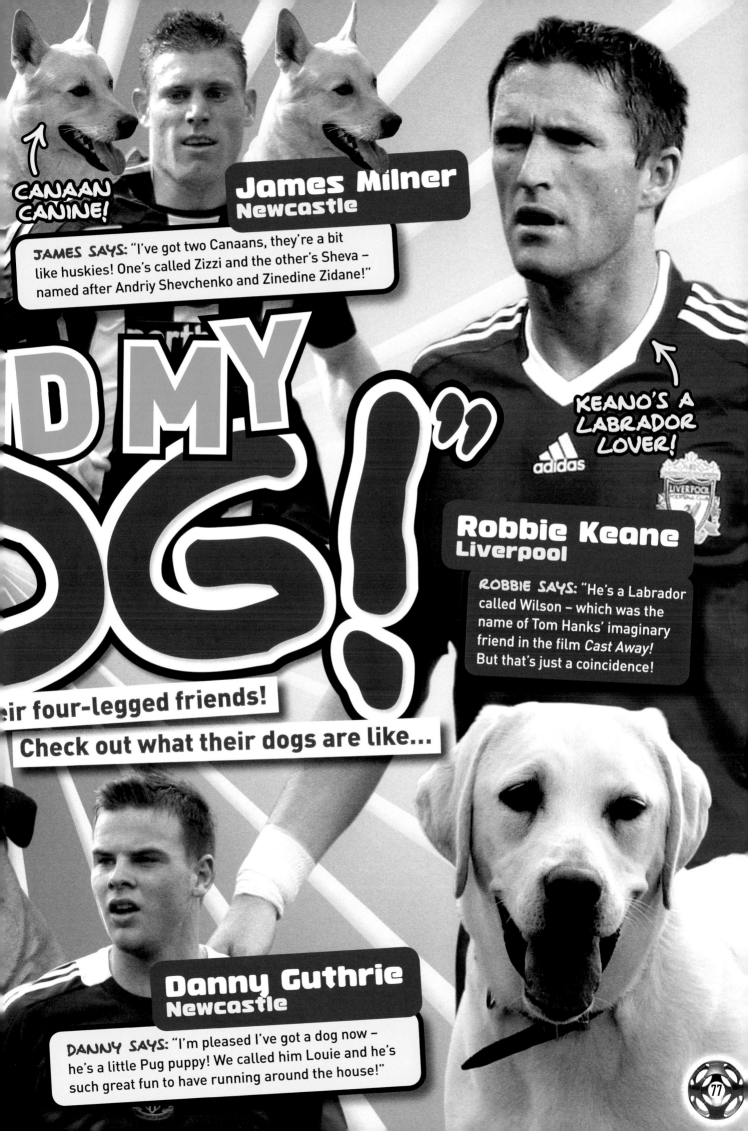

CANAAN CANINE!

James Milner
Newcastle

JAMES SAYS: "I've got two Canaans, they're a bit like huskies! One's called Zizzi and the other's Sheva – named after Andriy Shevchenko and Zinedine Zidane!"

D MY OG!"

KEANO'S A LABRADOR LOVER!

Robbie Keane
Liverpool

ROBBIE SAYS: "He's a Labrador called Wilson – which was the name of Tom Hanks' imaginary friend in the film *Cast Away*! But that's just a coincidence!"

eir four-legged friends!

Check out what their dogs are like...

Danny Guthrie
Newcastle

DANNY SAYS: "I'm pleased I've got a dog now – he's a little Pug puppy! We called him Louie and he's such great fun to have running around the house!"

MOTTY'S QUIZ! SPOT THE DIFFERENCE!

Circle the **5** differences between each pair of pictures and bag a point for each one you find!

MY SCORE... OUT OF **10**

MORE QUIZ FUN ON PAGE 84!

KEVIN NOLAN

BOLTON

PREMIER LEAGUE HERO!

Kev made his debut for the Trotters aged 17 – he's now played over 250 times for the club!

MATCH OF THE DAY MAGAZINE

Euro 200

Euro 2008 was a wicked footy party – check out Match

BEST PLAYER!

David Villa
Spain

SUPER VILLA!

The world's best stars rocked the show at Euro 2008. Deco, Xavi, Andrei Arshavin and Wesley Sneijder were all on fire, but it was super striker David Villa who was the star man – he hit the net four times to fire Spain into Euro heaven!

ARSHAVIN & SNEIJDER ROCKED TOO!

BEST CELEBRATION!

TUNCAY
v Czech Republic

The Turkey players went nuts when they came from 2-0 down to beat the Czech Republic. But no-one got as excited as Middlesbrough striker Tuncay – he jumped in the air and did a massive belly flop on all his team-mates! Ouch!

WHAT A COMEBACK!

BEST GAME!

Turkey v Czech Republic

There were some cracking games at Euro 2008 – Holland smashed their way past Euro big boys France and Italy with mega slick footy, but then Russia outclassed the Dutch with an amazing 3-1 win. Turkey trumped the lot, though, with their shock 3-2 comeback against the Czechs! They were awesome!

Awards!

TUNCAY FLOP!

SHOCK STAR!

Andrei Arshavin
Russia

We had a sneaky feeling that Arshavin was going to be a big star, but even we were shocked by his wicked skills – his deadly, darting runs caught out the best Euro defences and took the Russians all the way to the semis!

BEST TEAM!   Spain

Spain had everything in their squad to make them top Euro winners – their defence was rock solid, Xavi and Senna ruled the midfield, and Villa and Torres were the perfect strike duo. They even had super Cesc Fabregas to bring off the bench – what an amazing team!

RUSSIA'S BIG STAR!

UNSTOPPABLE!

TURN OVER

Euro 2008 Awards!

BIGGEST WHINGER!

Jens Lehmann
Germany

The German keeper didn't stop moaning at the Euros! He had a rant at Arsenal boss Arsene Wenger for not picking him, then tried to blame the ref for his team losing the final – even though Spain were miles better!

ZE BALL IS TOO ROUND!

BIGGEST GOON!

Luca Toni
Italy

Italy's number nine was in red-hot scoring form for Bayern Munich before the Euros, but as soon as he got to Austria and Switzerland he turned into a clumsy fool in front of goal – he looked like he'd never played footy before in his whole life!

FUNNIES

LUCA TONI?

JELLY?

BIGGEST BLUNDER!

Petr Cech
Czech Republic v Turkey

Mario Gomez missing two open goals for Germany was pretty bad, but Cech's howler against Turkey cost the Czechs a place in the quarters! All the keeper had to do was catch a simple cross – but he dropped it straight at Nihat's feet and he buried it! Oops!

BLOWN IT!

BEST GOAL!

Wesley Sneijder
Holland v Italy

One minute Holland were clearing an Italian chance off the line, the next they were steaming forward to score at breakneck speed! Van Bronckhorst swung in a deep cross, Kuyt headed back and Sneijder volleyed home for the perfect breakaway goal!

OOTY EXPERT!

BIG GIRL!

Mark Lawrenson

Lawro was cracking loads of gags at Euro 2008 – he even took the mickey out of the players in his commentary! He thought Luca Toni looked like a "six-foot jelly" and called Germany's giant centre-back Per Mertesacker a "big girl"!

BEST FANS!

Holland

HUMAN ORANGE!

ROARING DUTCHMAN!

We loved the mental fans dressing up to support their teams at Euro 2008 – the Dutch were the pick of the bunch! Every time their team played, they packed out the stadium like a giant orange – their costumes were completely crazy too!

CRAZIEST GAFFER!

Croatia's Slaven Bilic loved hopping up and down the touchline like a mad frog every time his team scored, but Fatih Terim of Turkey was the craziest! He went berserk at other gaffers, the ref, the fourth official and his own players – what a nutter!

HOPPING MAD!

NUTS!

Fatih Terim
Turkey

HOLLAND'S SPEED FOOTY!

MOTTY'S QUIZ!

10 QUESTIONS ON... NORTHERN IRELAND!

Grab a point for each one you get right!

1 True or false? Striker David Healy scored a hat-trick against Euro 2008 champions Spain in 2006!

YOU SAY ....

2 How old was superkid centre-back Jonny Evans when he made his debut?

YOU SAY ....

3 Which keeper has more caps – Roy Carroll or Maik Taylor?

YOU SAY ....

4 Steven Davis has played for two Prem clubs. Aston Villa is one – name the other.

YOU SAY ....

5 Who did Northern Ireland forward Chris Brunt win promotion with in 2008 – Stoke, Hull or West Brom?

YOU SAY ....

6 Which top Scottish club signed Northern Ireland winger Kyle Lafferty from Burnley in June 2008?

YOU SAY ....

7 True or false? Boss Nigel Worthington once won promotion to the Prem with Colchester!

YOU SAY ....

8 At which stadium do Northern Ireland play their home games?

YOU SAY ....

9 When was the last time Northern Ireland beat England – 1985, 1995, 2005?

YOU SAY ....

10 Which Championship team does midfielder Damien Johnson captain?

YOU SAY ....

MY SCORE... OUT OF 10

ANSWERS (DON'T CHEAT!)

1 True, 2 18, 3 Maik Taylor, 4 Fulham, 5 West Brom, 6 Rangers, 7 False, 8 Windsor Park, 9 2005, 10 Birmingham

MORE QUIZ FUN ON PAGE 92!

NICKY BARMBY

HULL CITY · F.C. · THE TIGERS

HULL CITY

Spain

EURO2008

CASILLAS!

FABREGAS!

TORRES!

WINNERS!

SIMON DAVIES

FULHAM

PREMIER LEAGUE HERO!

Simon scored wicked goals against Sunderland and Reading to help Fulham stay up last season!

MATCH OF THE **DAY**
MAGAZINE

WILSON PALACIOS

WIGAN

PENALTY SHO

COOL UNDER PRESSURE!

See if you can beat your mates with these five pens! Roll a dice – the number it lands on decides where the ball goes! (blue number = miss, red number = goal)

1

2

3

DEADLY FINISHER!

OT-OUT GAME!

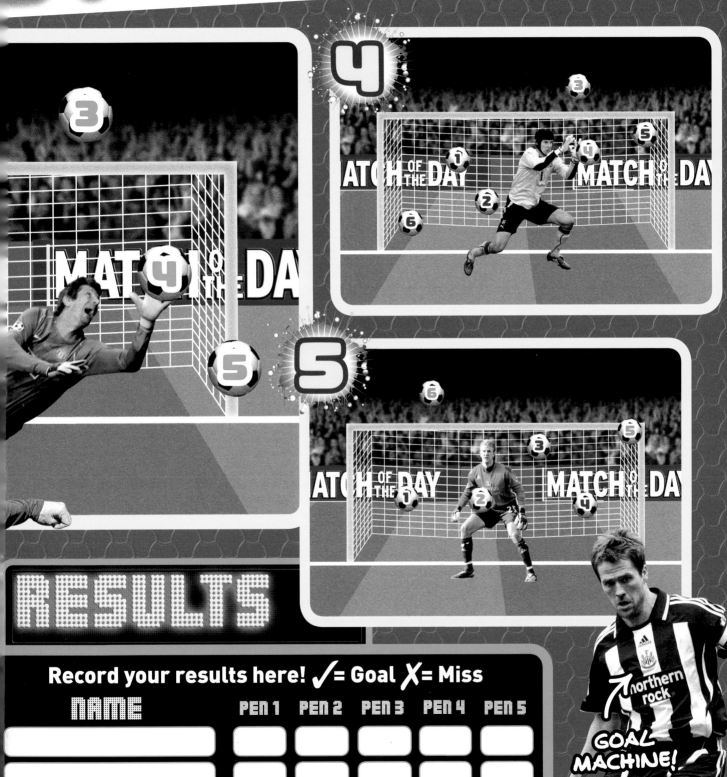

4

5 5

RESULTS

Record your results here! ✓= Goal ✗= Miss

NAME	PEN 1	PEN 2	PEN 3	PEN 4	PEN 5

GOAL MACHINE!

MOTTY'S QUIZ!
MYSTERY STARS!

Who are these **10** Prem players dressing up for the winter?

You get a point for each right answer!

1 ....

2 ....

3 ....

4 ....

5 ....

6 ....

7 ....

8 ....

9 ....

10 ....

MY SCORE... OUT OF **10**

TOTAL SCORE... **100**

92

Go to page 94 to see how you rate as a quiz king!

RICHARD CRESSWELL

STOKE

PREMIER LEAGUE HERO!

Richard netted 11 league goals last term to help Stoke reach the Prem for the first time ever!

MATCH OF THE **DAY** MAGAZINE

Motty's Quiz!

WHAT'S YOUR FINAL SCORE?

Add up your score from all ten quizzes to see your total out of 100!

0-20 POINTS FREE TRANSFER!

Oh no! Your footy knowledge is **a bit rubbish** and your boss has decided to release you from the club!

21-40 POINTS ON THE BENCH

Great news! The manager thinks you know **quite a bit about football** and brings you on from the subs bench!

Nice one! You're **well clued up** about the game and you bag your first goal in the Premier League!

41-60 POINTS GOAL HERO!

The fans think **you're awesome** because you can answer loads of tough questions. Brilliant stuff!

61-80 POINTS FANS' FAVE!

81-100 POINTS WORLD CLASS!

You're one of the best players on the planet! **There's not much you don't know about the game** – what a footy brainbox. Well done!